PATH TO THE GARDEN

Foundational Knowledge for the Believing Women & Men

Book I

Simplification of Primary (Islamic) Education for African Children

Book II

Motherly Advice for the Muslim Girl Conerning Religious and Worldly Life

By Shaykha Ruqayya bint Ibrahim Niass

First Published in 2015 by

Fayda Books, Publishing & Distribution
3695F Cascade Road
Atlanta, Georgia 30331

http://www.faydabooks.com
Email: orders@faydabooks.com

©Ruqyah bint Ibrahim Niass 2015

ISBN 978-0-9913813-7-1

No part of this book may be reproduced in any form without prior permission from copyright holder. All Rights Reserved

Cover Design
MUHAMMADAN PRESS

Printed and bound in the United States

BOOK I

Simplification of Primary Education for African Children

Preface

Shaykha Ruqayya Niass is a daughter of West Africa and also a renowned Islamic scholar. She was born on the night her father moved with his nascent community to Medina in the north of Kaolack (Sine-Saloum), at the end of 1930. Named after Ruqayya, the Prophet Muhammad's daughter, her father told her: "I named you Ruqayya, ascencion, since I have never ceased to ascend in the Divine Realm."

She learned Qur'an from her fathers Mauritanian disciple, Muhammad Rabbani. After committing the Holy Book to memory, she started learning fiqh from her father and arabic grammar from Ustadz Baye Ahmad Thiam (ajrumiyya, mulhatul i'rab, lamiyatul af'al). Later, she joined her fathers classes in alfiya, ihmirar and maqamat (assemblies of hariri) which took place in the early fifties. Before Shaykh Ibrahim would take over their teachings he submitted them to an exam in the following:

'Praise be to Allah who taught Man what he did not know. With that, I say to my bright children who excel in writing and in reasoning, who are bound for greatness. Follow the ways of greatness, for that is the best thing they can inherit from their parents. Let each of you right a report, in which he(or she) explains to me his(her) level of knowledge in arabic grammar."

At the same time, Shaykh sent a letter to Saydi Aliou Cisse and Baye Ahmad Thiam urging them to examine the reports written by his children (students) and to choose the best ones for an award. In that letter, shaykh ibrahim wrote a poem to be read to the students that would enlighten and galvanize their efforts. He said in it, referring to Shaykha Rokhaya Niass in 1951:

"I rejoice from your words like daughter like son, siblings you must be, do not be unjust toward yourselves."

The winners of the competition were Al hadj abdullah Niass (his first son), Shaykh Ruqayya Niass, Moustafa Diouf and Professor Ibrahim Mahmoud Diop.

In 1954, she wrote her first book called, Tanbihul bintul Muslimah (Motherly advice for the Muslim Girl...) which was commended by shaykh Ibrahim, Seydi Aliou Cisse, the Morrocan diplomat from Mauritania, the scholar Muhammad Kabir Ould Hurma Alawi, Ibrahim Mahmoud Diop and Muhammad Amin Ibrahim Niass.

The book enjoyed wide acclaim by critics and considered, by such authorities like Doctor Amar Samb, as the sole voice for women in 'senegalese arabic scholarship.

He translated the whole book into French, for his PhD dissertation in 1972 at Sorbonne university in Paris.

The first senegalese president, Leopold Sedar Senghor, although a christian, helped the Shaykh publish the book in the early sixties.

In the 1960's, she wrote the Taysir (Simplification of primary 'Islamic education) which is a simplified summarization of Islamic Foundational Knowledge, for the young boys and girls. It was supposed to be proposed as part of the curriculum in the Muslim primary school system.

The year 1975 was officially dedicated to women by the United Nations. At that UN convention a proclamation was signed for the elimination of all forms of discrimination against women.

Her father (Shaykh Ibrahim) ordered her to write a book about the position of women in Islam. Upon completion, she gave him the draft (which he approved before traveling to London where he passed on July 25th 1975). One of the Shaykhs students, the Former Nigerian Inspector general, M.D Yusuf, sponsored its publication in the early 80's.

The Shaykhas works are extensively quoted in university studies in Senegal as well as abroad. To name but a few... the PhD dissertation of professor Thierno Ka, the school of Pir Saniokhor, The scholarly paper titled 'Walking Qur'an' by Rudolph T. Ware, the article dedicated by ISESCO (Islamic Educational, Scientific and cultural organization). As for her works in Arabic and French, Zachary Valentine Wright, in included her in his PhD dissertation 'Embodied Knowledge', Evanston university.

She has also been a Muqaddamat (Propagator) in the Tijani Spiritual path since 1958. She received that full authorization (to Propagate the Tariqa) from her father (Shaykh Ibrahim Niass) while performing Hajj. He wrote the following prayer for her in the Ijaza (license to Propagate):

"May Allah bless anyone who takes knowledge from her, even if it is one single letter (of the alphabet)"

She was authorized by her father to call people to Islam with wisdom and good preaching. In a letter he wrote to her, while on her way to Nouackchott (Mauritania), he said:

"I forbid ignorant and greedy people to travel. As for you, you are authorized!, and wherever you set foot on, shall be a blessed place." This was written in 1971.

She has given the Shahada (Islamic Religion) to countless people in West Africa and thousands of people also took the Tijani litanies from her.

In short, Shaykha Ruqayya lives by the principles she wrote about all her life: Dedicate one's life to God and to mankind, shared her knowledge with her fellow sisters, enlighten the younger generation in life and religion.

She has participated in countless meetings and international conferences, in which she functions as the mouthpiece of Muslim women in Africa. Moreover, she has lectured in Europe (Stockholm, London, Manchester, Napoli...) about various topics such as women rights, religious intolerance, how to raise the economic capabilities of the African woman who are oftentimes the hands that feed the family.

With all of that, she never wavered in her duties as mother and wife. She was invited this year (2015) by the President Jimmy Carter Center in Atlanta, Georgia, to attend a worldwide forum on violence against women.

The Shaykha continues to work tirelessly, for the benefit of humanity.

This Preface was written by Cheikh Ahmad Boukar Niang (A son of the Shaykha)

Introduction

Praise belongs to Allah Who commanded us to learn what we do not know, the One Who said: *"Indeed only the scholars revere Allah among His servants"* **(Q35:28)**. Divine blessings and peace be upon Sayyidinâ Muhammad who said, "Seek knowledge even if you have to travel to China".

My dear brother Haj Abdullah son of Haj Ibrahim Niass commissioned me to compose a short book useful for the education of primary school children, which would include passages from the Holy Qur'an and Prophetic narrations, adhering to simple language to make it easy for children to comprehend and memorize. This booklet is the result of that request, and I ask Allah to realize his hope in me and make it a means of guidance for even one boy or girl, so that I may find great reward in the Presence of Allah Most High.

First Lesson: the Holy Qur'an

1. Opening Surah
2. Sura Ikhlas
3. sura falaq
4. sura naas
5. sura Sharh

Second Lesson

Allah is my Lord and Cherisher, Muhammad (saws) is my Prophet, Islam is my religion, the Ka'ba is my direction of focus in prayer, the Qur'an is my book of guidance, and the Muslims are my brothers.

Allah is my Lord and the Lord of all creatures, He is the One Who created me and created the universe and everything in it. He gives me life and takes life away.

Third Lesson

What are the first responsibilities upon the Muslim boy and girl?

It is necessary for all Muslim boys and girls to know that Allah Most High is his Lord and Creator, Provider and Guide, giving him life and taking it away. In this way, he will come to love Him and obey Him, and his heart will confirm His Oneness and recognize that He is characterized with Uniqueness, existing without beginning or end, completely different from non-eternal things, Self-Subsisting without need of others, Indivisible in His Essence and Qualities, All-Powerful, having effective Will, Knowledgeable, Hearing, Seeing, and Speaking. There is no god besides Him, glory be to Him Who fashions creatures in the womb as He wills.

Qul Huwa Allahu Ahad (**Q112:1-4**)

Laysa Ka mithlihi shay' (**Q42:11**): "There is nothing whatsoever like Him"

Fourth Lesson

Sayyidinâ Muhammad (blessings and peace upon him)

He is the Prophet sent to all of creation without exception, giving good news and warnings, calling to Allah by His permission, and an illuminating lamp.

From him we hope for intercession on the Day of Resurrection, and he is the ultimate intercessor for all of the servants by Divine permission. Allah said in His Book: *"Who can intercede before Him except by His Permission?"* **(Q2:255).**

He was born in Makka – may Allah bless him and grant him peace – at the time of dawn on Monday the 12th of the month of Rabi Awwal in the Year of the Elephant, at the hands of Sayyida Shifa the mother of Abdul Rahman ibn 'Auf. When he was delivered, he – blessings and peace be upon him – prostrated and then lifted his eyes to the heavens saying "O Allah, Most High and Sublime One!" He was delivered clean with his umbilical cord cut and circumcised... and his virtues cannot be counted!

Fifth Lesson

His upbringing (blessings and peace upon him)

Six years after his birth his mother passed away in Madina, and then he was cared for by his grandfather Abdul-Muttalib. When he was eight years old, his grandfather died, and his uncle Abu Talib began to look after him and preferred him over his own children. When he (blessings and peace be upon him) reached 12 years of age, he traveled with his uncle to Syria, and while there Buhayra – a Christian monk – recognized him as the awaited Prophet mentioned in the previous scriptures, and he informed Abu Talib of that and warned him against the Jews (who might attempt to harm his nephew). When he (blessings and peace be upon him) reached 25 years old, he married Khadija bint Khuwaylid.

Sixth Lesson

His ancestry (blessings and peace upon him)

Muslim boys and girls should know that the best and last of the Prophets is our master Muhammad – may Allah bless him and grant him peace, an Arab from the line of Bani Hashim – the noblest Arab tribe. He is: Muhammad son of Abdullah son of Abdul Muttalib son of Hashim son of Abd Manaf son of Qusayy son of Kilab son of Murra son of Ka'b son of Lu'ayy son of Ghalib son of Fihr son of Malik son of Nadr son of Kinana son of Khuzayma son of Mudrika son of Ilyas son of Mudar son of Nizar son of Ma'add son of 'Adnan. This ancestry traces back to Sayyidina Isma'il the son of Sayyidina Ibrahim – upon them be blessings and peace.

His mother is Amina bint Wahb son of Abd Manaf son of Zuhra son of Kilab.

One of the poets wrote:

"The fathers of the noblest of creation in ascending order -

He is the son of Abdullah (son of) Abdul Muttalib

Hashim Abd Manaf son of Qusayy -

son of Kilab Murra Ka'b and Lu'ayy

Ghalib son of Fihr son of Malik -

Nadr son of Kinanah as well

Khuzayma Mudrika Ilyas -

Mudar son of Nizar as is known

Then Ma'add and after him 'Adnan -

and after him the biographers differ in the details"

Seventh Lesson

His Children (blessings and peace of Allah be upon him)

He had seven children, 3 sons and 4 daughters. The males are: Abdullah, Qasim, and Ibrahim. The females are: Zaynab, Ruqayya, Um Kulthum, and Fatima.

The males all died while children. As for the females, all of them were alive during the Prophethood and became Muslim. All died during his life (blessings and peace be upon him) except for Sayyidah Fatima, who passed away six months after her father.

Eighth Lesson

His wives

Before he became a Messenger (blessings and peace be upon him), he married Khadija bint Khuwaylid, and she was the mother for all of his children except for Ibrahim – who was from Maria the Copt. After the passing of Khadija, he married numerous women, and at his passing he had nine wives. They were as follows: A'isha bint Abu Bakr, Hafsa bint Umar, Safiyya bint Huyay, Sawda bint Zam'a, Maymuna bint al-Harith, Um Salama Hind bint Abi Umaya, Zaynab bint Jahsh, Um Habiba Ramla bint Abi Sufyan, Juwayriya bint al-Harith. These are the mothers of the believers, who stood side by side with the men in all aspects of Islamic society, and were teachers to the women and many men as well... may Allah be pleased with them all! The Messenger of Allah (blessings and peace be upon him) said: "Women are the equal halves of men".

Ninth Lesson

His Successors (Khulafa) – Blessings and Peace be upon him

When the Messenger of Allah (Allah bless him and grant him peace) passed away, Abu Bakr as-Siddiq took charge of the affairs of the Muslims for nearly three years. After him Umar ibn al-Khattab led for ten years and six months, then after him Uthman ibn 'Affan for almost 13 years. After him, Ali ibn Abi Talib ruled for five years, (and then his son al-Hasan for six months). These are the rightly-guided successors who supported the Din and spread Islam and expanded its community into the lands of the Romans and Persians and others, may Allah be pleased with them all!

Tenth Lesson

The Migration

When the Messenger of Allah (blessings and peace upon him) was 52 years old, and the persecution from Quraysh became very severe and they intended to assassinate him, Allah Most High permitted him to emigrate to Madina, where most of its people had embraced Islam. So the Prophet left with Abu Bakr Siddiq, and when the people of Madina heard of their arrival, they went out to greet them with Takbir, and the women were striking the drums and singing in happiness:

The full moon rose upon us... (*Tala'al Badru 'Alayna...*)

For this reason they were titled "the Helpers" (Ansar), and the Islamic calendar begins at the date of the Prophet's migration to them (blessings and peace be upon him).

Muslim boys and girls should also know that Allah sent numerous Messengers before Sayyidina Muhammad, whom He chose and selected above all of mankind. Islam does not differentiate between any one of the Messengers in their mission. Hence, the role of Divinely sent Messenger is shared equally by our masters Nuh, Ibrahim, Musa, 'Isa, Yusuf, Ayyub, Salih, Shu'ayb, and so on, and Sayyidina Muhammad is among them and he is their seal and leader and the noblest of them.

Allah Most High said: "*You are the best of communities brought forth to the human race, you command the good and forbid the evil and believe in Allah*" (Q3:110) and "*Indeed We gave you the abundant good, so pray and sacrifice for your Lord, most assuredly he who despises you is cut-off*" (Q108:1-3) and "*How will it be when We bring forth from every community a witness, and bring you as a witness against these ones?*" **(Q4:41).**

Eleventh Lesson

The Book of Allah the Almighty

Muslim boys and girls must know that the Holy Qur'an is the Book of Allah and the Source of Law for the Muslims. By it they know what is true and what is false, and what is allowed and what is forbidden. They know that it is the revelation of Allah which falsehood can never approach – whether from the front or from the back – revealed by One Who is Wise and Praiseworthy. It is the Divine Everlasting constitution, therefore the Muslim must abide by its principles.

Its chapters number 114, ninety of them were revealed in Makka and twenty-four in Madina. It can be divided into 620 tenths, and its verses number 6,236. It contains 99,400 words and 321,670 letters. With each letter the reciter earns ten rewards. It contains fourteen places of prostration, and includes mention of 25 Prophets by name. The highest level of the Messengers are the Ulu'l 'Azm, who are: our masters Muhammad, Ibrahim, Nuh,

Musa, and 'Isa son of Maryam – blessings and peace be upon them all.

The Muslim boy and girl should also know that Makka is the sacred city and the Ka'ba is the ancient house of Allah. Allah said: *"I swear by the Fig and the Olive, and by the mount of Sinai, and by this sacred city, that We have created the human in the best of conformation..."* **(Q95:1-4).** Indeed, it is true, and we bear witness to that fact, that Allah the Great has spoken the truth!

Twelfth Lesson

The Necessity of Learning and the love of one's homeland

The Muslim boy and girl must understand that helping each other in righteousness and taqwa is an obligation upon us Muslims, as the Messenger (upon him be blessings and peace) said: "Allah continues to aid the servant so long as the servant continues to aid his brother". And Allah Most High said: "*Aid each other in righteousness and taqwa and do not aid each other in sin and rebellion*" (Q5:2).

The Muslim boy and girl should also know that learning and increasing knowledge is also an obligation, because Allah said: "*It is only the scholars among His servants who truly revere Allah*" (**Q35:28**) and the Messenger said: "Seek knowledge even if you need to go to China". It is also commonly known that whatever you learn while young stays with you as inscriptions stay in stone.

The Muslim child should also love his homeland, because this is part of belief, as has been narrated from the Prophet (blessings and peace be upon him).

When he grows a little older he should begin gaining experience in a skill or trade so that he may earn a living, keeping in mind the Prophetic advice: "Work for this lower world as if you will live forever, and work for the next world as if you will die tomorrow".

Thirteenth Lesson

The Revelation of the Qur'an

The Qur'an is the Book revealed by Allah to Sayyidina Muhammad in the cave of Hira with the agency of angel Jibril (upon him be peace), who said to him, "Read!" and he replied, "I am not a reader". So the angel asked him a second and third time, each time squeezing the Prophet tightly, until he asked, "what shall I read?". Then the angel said, *"Read in the Name of your Lord Who created, created the human from a blood-clot, read and your Lord is the most Generous, He Who taught by the pen, taught the human what he did not know..."* (**Q96:1-5**). Sayyidina Muhammad (blessings and peace upon him) was given revelation with Iqra' (Read) and given the task of Messenger-hood with sura Mudathir.

The Qur'an continued to be revealed piece by piece until the whole Mushaf was completed, as a book of Divine guidance and clarification for humankind.

Fourteenth Lesson

Islam and the Ka'ba

Islam is the religion of truth, as Allah said: "*Indeed, the religion acceptable with Allah is Islam*" **(Q3:19)** and "*I have chosen with pleasure Islam as your Din*" **(Q5:3)**. The Din of Islam has principles and foundations.

The Ka'ba is the sacred house of Allah which is in the blessed city of Makka. Allah said: "*Summon the people to Hajj, they will come walking and riding upon lean camels, traveling from every deep canyon, to partake of Divine favors laid out for them*" **(Q22:27).** And Allah said to Sayyidina Muhammad: "*We see the turning of your face to the sky, and We will direct you to a Qibla which pleases you, so direct your face towards the Sacred Mosque*" **(Q2:144).**

Fifteenth Lesson

Concerning Ritual Purity

Allah Most High said: "*O believers, when you stand up to pray wash your faces, and your hands up to the elbows, and wipe your heads, and your feet up to the ankles. If you are defiled, purify yourselves; but if you are sick or on a journey, or if any of you comes from the restroom, or you have touched women, and you can find no water, then have recourse to wholesome dust and wipe your faces and your hands with it. God does not desire to make any impediment for you; but He desires to purify you, and that He may complete His blessing upon you; that you may be thankful.*" **(Q5:6).**

Sixteenth Lesson

the Five Pillars of Islam

They are as follows: to testify that there is no deity but Allah and that Sayyidina Muhammad is His final messenger, to establish the prayer, to pay the zakat, to fast Ramadan, and to perform the pilgrimage for those who are able.

The meaning of the first pillar – the testification – is to believe in the heart and affirm with the tongue, that there is no one worthy of worship other than Allah Most High, and that Sayyidina Muhammad is the Messenger of Allah and the seal of the Prophets. He (Most High) said: *"Allah testifies that there is no god but He"* **(Q3:18),** and: *"There has come to you a Messenger from among yourselves, grievous to him is your suffering, he is concerned for you, to the believers is he kind and merciful"* **(Q9:128),** and: *"We have not sent you except as a mercy to all the worlds"* **(Q21:107).**

Seventeenth Lesson

The Ritual Prayer (Salat) and the Alms (Zakat)

Salat is a specific form of worship performed in a specific manner. Its importance can be seen in the statement of Allah Most High: *"Regularly guard your prayers, especially the middle prayer, and be upright in obedience before Allah"* (**Q2:238**), and *"The believers are indeed successful, those who are humbly present in their prayers"* (**Q23:1-2**). The Messenger of Allah (blessings and peace be upon him) said: "Prayer is the support of the Din and the core of worship".

As for Zakat: it is defined as a specific form of wealth taken out of a specific form of wealth, when it reaches a specific lower limit, and is given to specific recipients at specified times. The conditions for its obligation are three: freedom (from slavery), the full ownership of the minimum threshhold, and the passing of a full lunar year over that minimum. Allah Most High said: *"It is He who produces gardens trellised, and untrellised, palm-trees, and crops diverse in produce, olives, pomegranates, like each to each, and each unlike to each. Eat of their fruits when they fructify, and pay the due thereof on the day of its harvest"* (**Q6:141**).

Eighteenth Lesson

The obligation of fasting (Sawm) and pilgrimage (Hajj)

Linguistically fasting means to abstain, and in the religious context it means to abstain completely from eating and drinking and sexual relations from dawn until sunset throughout the entire month of Ramadan. The ideal is that the one who fasts is supposed to abstain from all that is other than Allah Most High. He said: *"Fasting has been prescribed upon you as it has been on those before you, that you may attain godwariness (taqwa)"* **(Q2:183)**.

Pilgrimage linguistically means to go after a goal, and in the religious context means a series of acts of worship and rites that include entering a state of sacredness, circumambulation, walking between two mounts, standing on the plain of 'Arafa, and other sacred rites. The conditions for its obligation are five, namely: reaching and passing the onset of puberty, having a sound mind, freedom from slavery, financial and physical ability, and being a Muslim.

Nineteenth Lesson

Concerning Belief (Imân) and Spiritual Excellence (Insân)

Belief (Iman) refers to having complete conviction in the existence of Allah Most High, and in the validity of the Divine books, messengers, angels, the last day, the Divine decree of destiny (its good and bad, sweet and bitter), in paradise and hell-fire, in the bridge of the hereafter, and in the Basin (Hawd) of the Prophet (blessings and peace be upon him).

Spiritual Excellence refers to worshipping Allah in such a way as if you see Him directly, knowing that He sees and watches you. The Din of Islam is all these three: Islam, Iman, and Ihsan. Allah Most High said: *"The Messenger believes in the revelations to him from his Lord, as do the believers; all of them believe in Allah and His angels and His scriptures and His Messengers, saying, 'we do not discriminate between any of the messengers' 'we hear and obey, we seek Your forgiveness our Lord, and to You is the ultimate end'!"* **(Q2:285)**.

Review Exercises:

- What is the testimony of Islamic faith?
- What is Salat?
- What is Zakat?
- What is Sawm?
- What is Hajj?
- What is Iman?
- What is Ihsan?
- Have any verses of the Qur'an discussed these meanings?

"We indeed revealed this on the night of Decree, and what will explain to you what is the night of Decree? The night of Decree is better than a thousand months. The angels and the Spirit descend in it by permission of their Lord upon every command. Peace it is, until the rising of dawn" **(Q97:1-5).**

Twentieth Lesson

On Ritual Purity (Tahara) and the Types of Water

Ritual purity is of two types: purity from ritual filth (hadath), and purity from physical filth (khabath). Both of these types of purity must be present before one can be allowed to pray (or carry the Qur'an or go on Pilgrimage). It can only be achieved by pure and purifying water, meaning water in its absolute sense and natural definition without qualifiers (e.g. Like rose-water). Otherwise, water which is mixed can either be mixed with a pure substance or impure one.

Water which is mixed with an impure substance has three judgments: 1) a small amount of water and small amount of impurity: it is disliked to perform Wudu' with this; 2) a small amount of water and large amount of impurity: it is not allowed to use this for Wudu'; and 3) a large amount of water with some impurity: it is not disliked to use this for Wudu'.

As for water mixed with a pure substance, it has two judgments: 1) something which can be easily avoided, such as

Saffron, oil, fat, yeast, etc... if this changes one of the three properties of water (color, taste, smell), then it is considered pure but not purifying, and it can only be used for daily tasks like cooking or drinking; or 2) what cannot easily be avoided, including pure things found in the habitat of the water, like moss or algae or sulfur; in this case the water is pure and purifying and can be used for ritual purification.

Review Exercises:
- What is ritual purity (tahara)?
- What is ritual filth (hadath)?
- What is physical filth (khabath)?
- What is natural water?
- What is mixed water and its types?
- What are some Qur'anic verses speaking about ritual purity?

Twenty First Lesson

Ritual purification (Wudu')

An obligation (farida) is defined as an action which carries reward if you do it and punishment if you do not.

The mandatory elements of Wudu' are seven:

- the intention (niyyah), which should be formed at or right before washing the face. The "face" is defined as the circle encompassed by the normal hairline on top to the tip of the beard on bottom (and the right and left earlobes).
- Washing the face
- washing the forearms up to and including the elbows
- wiping the head
- washing the feet up to and including the ankles
- doing these in immediate succession with no gaps in time
- passing the hands (or other limb) over the specific body part during or directly after the contact with water

- The stressed recommendations (Sunna) of Wudu' are seven:
- washing the hands up to the wrists before placing them into the water container
- swishing and spitting the water from the mouth
- slightly inhaling some water through the nostrils and blowing it out
- the return wipe over the head (from behind to front)
- wiping the ears (front and back side)
- taking new water for each step
- doing the mandatory elements of Wudu' in order (as described above)

The Sunna here is defined as what the Prophet (blessings and peace on him) did in front of others without indicating that it is an obligation.

The meritorious acts of Wudu' are seven:
- uttering the Basmala before commencing
- performing Wudu' in a clean place
- placing the water container on the right side of the body if it has an open top; otherwise keeping it on the left side
- the second repetition
- the third repetition
- cleaning the right limb before the left one
- using the tooth-stick (Miswak)

During Wudu' you must make sure when washing the face to include the wrinkles and deep spots around the eyes and so on, and the bridge between the nostrils, and the out part of the lips, and other such parts that are sometimes forgotten.

The conditions of obligation: reaching the state of puberty, and the ability to perform the acts of Wudu' and to use water, being sure or having strong doubt that one has nullified a previous Wudu' (meaning in a state of ritual impurity), and the time of prayer coming in.

The conditions of validity: being a Muslim, having no barriers to the water reaching the limbs and body parts, and there being no nullifier for it.

The conditions of both obligation and validity: being of sound mind, being presented with an authentic description of the Prophetic message, for women to be done with the blood of menstruation or post-natal bleeding, having access to enough water, and not being asleep or unconscious.

It is also necessary during Wudu' to go between the fingers of the hand, while going between the toes is recommended; and if the beard is thin and see through one must insert the wet hands through the hairs, otherwise that is not necessary.

At the conclusion of Wudu' it is recommended to utter the following invocation:

ashhadu al-la ilaha illa-Allah wahdahu la sharika lahu, wa ashhadu anna Muhammadan 'abduhu wa rasuluh, allahumma ij'alni min at tawwabin waj'alni min al mutaTahhirin, waj'alni min 'ibadik as-Salihin. (I testify that there is no god but Allah, One without a partner, and I testify that Muhammad is His servant and messenger, O Allah make me one of the repenters, and one of the purifiers, and one of Your righteous servants).

Review Exercises:
- What are the mandatory elements of Wudu'?
- What are the stressed recommendations of Wudu'?
- What are the conditions of Wudu'?
- When is it necessary to take the water between the fingers, and when is it recommended?
- What does one say after finishing Wudu'?

(Surat Takathur)

Twenty Second Lesson

What Nullifies Wudu'

Acts of Ritual Impurity (Hadath): three from the front genitals and two from the back

- urine
- pre-ejaculate sexual fluid
- wady, which is a thick white-colored liquid that usually exits after urinating
- passing gas
- feces

Secondary causes (Asbab):
- Sleeping, which has three judgments: 1) long deep sleep: this nullifies Wudu'; 2) long light sleep: it is recommended to renew Wudu'; 3) short light sleep: this does not nullify Wudu.

- Altered mental state: this is where one loses his or her mind either due to insanity or coma or fainting, or becoming intoxicated
- Leaving Islam to another religion
- Having doubts about performing Wudu' or not (for one who does not usually suffer from doubts)
- Kissing the opposite gender on the mouth, or kissing with sensual pleasure (not simply kissing to say goodbye or out of mercy)
- Touching the opposite gender with the intention or experience of sensual pleasure
- The man touching the penis with the palm or inside of one's fingers, either purposefully or accidentally (not the back of one's hand).

Twenty Third Lesson

Dry Ablution (Tayammum)

Tayammum is to wipe the face and hands with clean earth (or mud or marsh or sand etc.) instead of wet ablution (Wudu'). It does not remove the ritual impurity, but only gives permission to perform physical worship. With each act of tayammum you can only perform one obligatory prayer. It is not allowed to use glass or wood or grass or bricks or mats or carpets. However, an ill person may use stone.

The circumstances that make it permissible to use tayammum are: not having water, being unable to use water, having a sickness that precludes use of water, fearing the time of prayer may finish and having access to clean earth (in which case one does tayammum instead of using up the remaining time in Wudu'). Tayammum has the same nullifiers as Wudu', with the addition of finding water before the time of Salat ends.

The obligatory elements of tayammum are five: the intention to allow an act of worship (including the intention to remove greater impurity – Janaba – if needed), striking the earth the first time with the hands, covering the entire face, covering the hands including the wrists and between the fingers, and doing that in uninterrupted succession.

Twenty Fourth Lesson

Major Purification Bath (Ghusl)

This is defined as the washing of the entire body from the tip of the head to the tip of the toes, as a result of having major impurity (janaba) from performing sexual intercourse or ejaculation (whether asleep or awake) or from menstruation or post-natal bleeding.

The required elements are five: having the specific intention, covering the entire body with water, passing a limb (or cloth or towel) over the whole body, reaching the roots of the hair with water, and performing all the steps in uninterrupted succession (if able).

The stressed recommendations are four: washing the hands with the wrists, rinsing the mouth with water (swish and spit), cleaning the nose by gently inhaling with water then exhaling, and gently wiping the ears (taking care not to harm them by using too much water).

The meritorious actions are six: beginning with the removal of any physical filth, starting with the top of the body and limbs before the bottom, and with the right before the left, washing the head hair 3 times, using as little water as needed while making a complete ghusl, and performing a wudu' along with the ghusl as part of it.

Twenty Fifth Lesson

The Ritual Prayer (Salât)

Linguistically Salat means prayer and mercy, while in the religious context it refers to an act of worship that contains an opening Takbir, recitation of Qur'an, prostration, and a greeting of peace to exit, and it has conditions. The conditions of obligation are: the onset of puberty, and not being forced against one's will to abandon it.

The conditions of validity are five: being pure and free from any ritual or physical filth, facing your body towards the Qibla, avoiding many extraneous motions, covering one's nakedness (if able), and being a Muslim. The nakedness of a man is defined here as the area covering between the navel and the knees, and of a woman is defined as everything except her face and hands. Otherwise, both male and female are perfectly able to achieve human perfection.

The conditions of both validity and obligation are six: the ceasing of menstrual or post-natal blood for women, receiving an authentic representation of the Message of Islam, having a sound mind, having access to enough water, lack of sleep or absentmindedness, and entrance of the time of prayer.

Basmala – Surat 'Asr **(Q103:1-3)**.

Twenty Sixth Lesson

The obligatory elements (fara'id) and stressed recommendations (sunnan) of the Salat

They are 13 in number:

- forming a solid intention during the opening takbir ("Allahu Akbar")
- the opening takbir
- standing while uttering the opening takbir
- recitation of the Fatiha
- standing during the recitation of the Fatiha
- bowing at the waist (ruku')
- standing back straight from it
- the two prostrations
- sitting up from it
- closing the prayer with the greeting of peace (Salam)
- sitting for the Salam

- having throughout the prayer a state of focused tranquility and presence

Some scholars added an extra one which is to specify in the intention what type of prayer it is and whether one intends to follow behind an imam.

As for the stressed recommendations, they are 12 in number:

- the addition surah after the Fatiha in the first two cycles, for the Imam and one praying alone
- standing while reciting the surah
- reciting at a low volume (like a whisper) during the day prayers (except for the Imam in Jumu'a)
- reciting at a higher audible volume for the night prayers (Fajr, Maghrib, Isha, Witr)
- every Takbir besides the opening one
- Saying "Sami'allahu liman Hamidah", by the Imam and the one praying alone
- the first sitting for tashahud after two cycles
- the last sitting at the end enough to utter the closing greeting of peace, and the return greeting (done by the follower in group prayer)
- the first tashahud and tahiyyat
- the second/final one
- having a barrier (sutra) in front of one while praying
- the follower in group prayer giving the salam to the one on his/her left

The meritorious acts of Salat are as follows:
- Raising the hands during the opening takbir

- lengthening the recitation of the Subh and Dhuhr prayers
- shortening the recitation of the 'Asr and Maghrib prayers
- having the length of recitation of the 'Isha prayer be in between the above
- saying Rabbana wa Laka'l Hamd after rising from bowing
- the phrases of glorification (tasbih) during bowing and prostration
- saying Amin after the Fatiha
- the du'a of Qunut

Twenty Seventh Lesson

The Wording of the Tashahud

The traditional wording of the Tashahud is as follows:

at-Tahiyyatu lillah, az-Zakiyatu lillah, at-Tayyibat as-Salawat lillah, as-Salamu ʿalayka ayyuha-n Nabi wa rahmatullahi wa barakatuh, as-Salamu ʿalayna wa ʿala ʿibad illah is-Salihin, ashhadu al-la ilaha illa-llahu wahdahu la sharika lahu, wa ashhadu anna Muhammadan ʿabduhu wa rasuluh.

This is followed by the Salawat Ibrahimiya:

Allahumma Salli ʿala sayyidina Muhammad wa ʿala Ali sayyidina Muhammad, kama sallayta ʿala Sayyidina Ibrahim wa ʿala Ali sayyidina Ibrahim, wa Barik ʿala Sayyidina Muhammad wa ʿala Ali Sayyidina Muhammad kama Barakta ʿala Sayyidina Ibrahim wa ʿala Ali Sayyidina Ibrahim fi'l ʿAlamin innaka Hamidun Majid.

Twenty Eighth Lesson

the wording of the Qunut Du'a

The supplication (du'a) of Qunut is said in the second cycle of Subh prayer, before bowing. The traditional wording is:

Allahumma Inna Nasta'inuka wa nastaghfiruka wa nu'minu bika wa natawakkalu 'alayk, wa nuthni 'alayk al khayra kullah, nashkuruk wa la nakfuruk, wa nakhna'u laka wa nakhla'u wa natruku man yafjuruk, Allahumma iyyaka na'bud wa laka nusalli wa nasjud, wa ilayka nas'aa wa nahfid, narju rahmatak wa nakhafu 'adhabak al-jidd, inna 'adhabak bil kafirina mulhiq.

(O Allah! We ask Your help and Your forgiveness, We believe in You and rely upon You, and praise You with all the good You deserve, We thank you and are not ungrateful to You, We submit to You and leave and abandon those who transgress against You. O Allah, You do we worship and for You do we pray and prostrate, and to You do we run and aspire, we hope in Your mercy and fear Your severe punishment, indeed Your punishment is surrounding the non-believers).

During the bowing, the phrase of glorification is: **Subhana Rabbi al'Adhim wa bi-Hamdih**

During the prostration it is: **Subhana Rabbi al-A'la wa bi-Hamdih.**

Twenty Ninth Lesson

the Disliked and Offensive Acts (Makruh) during the Salât

The acts that are disliked to perform while praying are:

- supplication (Du'a) after the opening takbir or during recitation of Qur'an or while bowing or in the first tashahud or after the Imam offers his concluding Salam
- prostrating upon clothes or carpets or the lose part of a turban or one's sleeve
- to intertwine one's fingers or crack one's knuckles
- to recite Qur'an while bowing or prostrating
- closing one's eyes (unless one is avoiding a specific visual distraction)
- putting the hands on the waist
- putting one foot upon another
- thinking about worldly affairs

- the eyes going here and there
- playing with one's beard or hair or clothes, because one is standing before Allah Most High
- holding something in one's mouth or sleeve
- saying the ta'awudh (a'udhu billahi min ash-shaytan ir-rajim) before the Fatiha or Sura in the obligatory prayer
- repeating the same surah in the first two cycles of an obligatory prayer
- reciting more than one surah in a single cycle of an obligatory prayer

Qur'an (16:78-79, 81): *"and Allah brought you out from your mother's womb and you had no knowledge, and He provided you with hearing and vision and hearts, so that you may be grateful. Do they not consider the birds flying in the sky, held up by none other than Allah? Indeed, in that there are signs for those who believe... and Allah provided for you shade from the sun, and dwellings in the mountains, and clothes which protect you from the elements and armor to wear which protects you from your weapons. In such a way does He complete His favor upon you, so that you may show gratitude".*

Thirtieth Lesson

Acts which Nullify the Salat

They are four in number:

- Purposefully speaking words not part of the Prayer
- 3 or more extraneous actions or movements
- eating or drinking
- forgetting or dropping one of the conditions or obligatory elements

The person praying must understand that he/she is standing before Allah Most High and conversing with Him. The Salat contains a light which illuminates the hearts of the worshippers, and it expands the breast and distances from sin. Salat is also a beneficial physical exercise. Therefore, every adult Muslim of sound mind should be keen as to its performance and not treat it lightly. The people of the Fire were asked, "What made you enter the Hell-fire?" and they replied, "We used to not pray...". It is the responsibility of the guardian of the child to command him/her to pray when they reach seven years of age. If at the end of ten years the child still does not pray, the guardian should discipline him.

Practice Surah: (Surah Fil – Q105: 1-5).

Thirty First Lesson

The Specific Times when it is disliked to pray

It is not allowed to pray while the sun's disc is rising or setting on the horizon, or during the Friday speech. It is disliked to pray after the Subh prayer until the moment when the sun is at an angle above the horizon (usually between 20-40 minutes), and between 'Asr prayer and the setting of the sun, and between sunset and Maghrib prayer.

If anyone out of forgetfulness adds an extra act during the prayer, he should perform two prostrations of forgetfulness after the concluding Salam. If one forgets an obligatory element and remembers while in prayer, or he forgot to do a sunna of the prayer, he should perform that and then do two prostrations of forgetfulness before the concluding salam. If he both forgot and added something, he should perform those two prostrations before the concluding salam.

Thirty Second Lesson

The prayers that are highly stressed (sunna mu'akkada)

These include the Witr (single unit) prayer at the end of the night, the two 'Eid communal prayers, the solar and lunar eclipse prayer, and the drought prayer. As for the two cycles of Fajr sunna before the Subh prayer, they are a Raghiba (in between Sunna and Nafl) and can be made up until midday. Also, praying the mandatory prayers (aside from Jumu'ah) in a group is a stressed sunna for resident males.

As for the Friday prayer (Jumu'ah), praying it as a group is one of its conditions of validity. The other conditions of validity for the group prayer are: that the Imam be a Muslim male post-puberty and of sound mind, and knowledgeable of the rules of prayer, and that the follower intends to be a follower of this Imam in the prayer.

Thirty Third Lesson

the Friday prayer (Jumu'ah)

The Jumu'ah prayer is an individual obligation upon all male free resident Muslims (who don't have a valid excuse to miss it). The conditions of its validity are: being a permanent resident in the location, having at least twelve males in the congregation aside from the resident Imam, the two speeches that precede the Prayer that the Imam must deliver while standing, and that it be performed in the city's central masjid (built like the other normal buildings of the city and not at a lower quality). It must also occur after midday and the speeches must be given before the prayer. According to Imam Malik, there are no specific limits for the speeches; rather they should be anything that the Arabs would classify as a formal speech.

Thirty Fourth Lesson

the Etiquettes of Jumu'ah and valid excuses to miss it

Its etiquettes are as follows:

- performing a Ghusl for it, which is a stressed sunna
- brushing one's teeth and trimming one's nails
- avoiding anything that can create a bad odor
- wearing nice clothes and perfume for it
- walking to the masjid is preferable unless that is difficult

The excuses which permit one to not attend are:

- severe weather
- leprosy and other similar ailments that have strong body odor
- oneself being sick
- a close relative – such as a spouse or parent – being sick and no one else is around who can tend to them

- a close relative in the last moments of life
- someone who is afraid of being caught by an unjust ruler and putting him in jail or taking his property
- someone who is unable to pay back a loan and is afraid that the creditor will catch him and jail him
- a blind person who has no one to lead him or cannot guide himself to the masjid.

Thirty Fifth Lesson

What is disliked and prohibited during Jumu'ah

It is prohibited on Friday for resident Muslim males to:

- travel at midday on Friday and miss the prayer
- speak or pray voluntary prayers while the Imam is giving the speech
- to buy or sell after the second Adhan (and any such transaction is void and invalid)

It is disliked to:

- for the Imam to pray voluntary prayers before the speech
- for the follower to pray voluntary prayers after the first Adhan
- for the young lady to attend the prayer
- to travel out of town after dawn on Friday and miss the Jumu'ah

The Imam leading the Jumu'ah prayer must be an adult and resident, as it is not allowed for a pre-pubescent boy or a traveler to lead it. Also, the one who gives the speech should also lead the prayer, unless he has a valid excuse.

Thirty Sixth Lesson

Items from which Alms (Zakat) is due

Zakat is obligatory upon three categories of wealth: livestock/cattle, crops, and currency.

For grazing livestock, only camels, cows, bulls, sheep and goats apply, not other types (horses, chicken, etc). Zakat on them becomes due once a certain minimum threshold (nisab) of cattle head are reached, and once a full lunar year passes. For camels, the minimum threshold is five camels, from which one sheep is due. For cows, the minimum is 30 cows, from which one calf that entered its third year is due. For sheep and goats (considered one group), the minimum threshold is 40 head of at least one year old, from which one sheep is due. There are more details for numbers beyond these.

As for crops, the only condition is having a quantity of ripe crops that meet the minimum threshold. The crops must be those which can be stored for a long time without spoiling, and able to be staple nourishment. The minimum threshold is equal to 609 liters net weight, from which ten percent is due if rainwater is used to irrigate the fields, and five percent is irrigation is done mechanically or human effort. (If both, then 7.5% is due).

As for currency, this refers to gold and silver, and can also refer to any other currency that takes their place. The minimum threshold for gold is 20 dinars, and for silver is 200 dirhams. Note that gold and silver jewelry in private possession of the female does not have Zakat due upon it, only gold and silver that is used for business. The amount due is 2.5% of whatever total amount of currency there is, after one full year passing starting from the point the currency was first acquired, as long as throughout the year it never dipped below the minimum threshold.

Thirty Seventh Lesson

Zakat al-Fitr

This is a second type of mandatory Zakat due at the end of Ramadan on Eid al-Fitr. Every legally responsible Muslim – male or female – who has extra wealth above what they and their dependents need on the day of Eid, must pay this Zakat. The amount to be paid is 3 liters of the main staple food of the location, and it becomes due either on the last Maghrib of Ramadan or on dawn the day of Eid.

Zakat in general is to only be paid to the following categories of recipients:

- the poor, those who do not have enough money for a year
- the destitute, who do not have enough money for a day
- zakat collectors, even if they are rich
- to free slaves
- those who newly embraced Islam

- those who are unable to pay debts that are due
- soldiers in Jihad
- a traveler who is short on money

Thirty Eighth Lesson

on Fasting (Sawm)

It means to abstain from eating or drinking and sexual relations from the beginning of dawn until the complete setting of the sun, all the days of Ramadan. It is obligatory upon every Muslim of sane mind and post-puberty who is physically able and (for women) are not menstruating or having post-natal bleeding.

Its obligatory elements are: to form a solid intention the night before that one will fast that following day, and abstaining from anything that would annul the fast, such as ingesting food or drink or intentional vomiting or menstruating or post-natal bleeding or abandoning Islam or losing one's sanity.

Thirty Ninth Lesson

the stressed recommendations (sunnan) of fasting

These sunan are:
- delaying the pre-dawn meal (suhoor) as much as possible before Fajr; the Messenger of Allah (blessings and peace be upon him) said: "Eat suhoor for it has blessing".
- eating the break-fast meal (iftar) as early as possible after Maghrib
- breaking the fast with dates or with water if no dates, as he (blessings and peace be upon him) said: "If one of you eats after fasting, let him begin with dates, or if there are no dates then with water, for these are purification".
- To busy one's time with recitation of Qur'an and dhikr, for he (blessings and peace be upon him) said: "Whoever does not desist from evil speech and wrong action

during fasting, then Allah pays no importance to him leaving food and drink".

There are also disliked and offensive things to do during fasting, such as:

- tasting a food with the tip of the tongue
- chewing gum
- smelling perfume
- foul speech

It is permitted for the sick to not fast if he fears any bodily harm from fasting, as well as for a traveler who is traveling more than 50 miles. Both of them are required to make up those missed days by fasting other days, according to the words of the Messenger of Allah (blessings and peace be upon him), when one Sahabi asked him about fasting during travel: "Not fasting during travel is a concession granted by Allah, so whoever takes it it is fine, and whoever still desires to fast there is no blame on him".

The pregnant and breastfeeding are also excused from fasting if they fear any bodily harm for themselves or their child, and they must make up the days missed.

It is also permitted for the very old and frail people who cannot fast, or for someone with terminal illness, to not fast and instead feed poor people, equal to one meal of half-liter for each day skipped, and there is no requirement to make it up later.

The women who are menstruating or having post-natal bleeding are not allowed to fast, and they have to make up those days once they are blood-free. If someone does not fast and has no excuse, they not only have to make up that day but also perform an expiation of fasting 60 consecutive days or feeding sixty poor people.

Five days of the year it is prohibited to fast: the two days of Eid, and the three days following the Eid al-Adha. It is also not allowed to fast on the "day of doubt" which is the last day of Sha'ban that could be Ramadan, unless it falls on someone's habitual day of fasting.

If someone during a Ramadan fast unintentionally eats, then there is no requirement to make it up (in some madhabs), and they should just continue the remainder of the day fasting. This is according to the hadith: "Whoever mistakenly eats during Ramadan, then there is no requirement to make it up or perform an expiation". Likewise, whoever vomits unintentionally does not have to make up that day, but whoever intentionally induces vomit then the fast is broken and he must make it up.

Fortieth Lesson

on Pilgrimage (Hajj)

Pilgrimage refers to going to the Sacred Ka'ba and surrounding areas to perform specific sacred rites at specified times, and it has a number of required integrals and obligatory elements without which the Hajj would be invalid.

The integrals are five:
- for the men to strip from normal clothes and enter the sacred state by wearing the Ihram garment, which is two large un-sewn garments, with the intention to perform one of the types of Hajj.
- Standing upon the plain of 'Arafa for a part of the night
- circumambulating around the Ka'ba seven times
- going seven times between Safa and Marwa
- shaving or trimming the head-hair

The obligatory elements are also five:
- to enter into the sacred state of Ihram from one of the five specified points of entry (Miqat)
- to cast the stones against the three pillars
- sleeping in Mina during the days of Tashreeq
- sleeping in Muzdalifa
- abstaining from the prohibited acts during Ihram, which include covering the hair (or head) for men or covering the face for women, wearing sewn garments, combing or oiling hair, trimming fingernails, removing body hair, applying perfume, and hunting.

The stressed recommendations (sunan) of Hajj are many. They include:
- performing a Ghusl bath for Ihram and before standing at 'Arafa and for casting the stones
- applying perfume before Ihram
- wearing two white new un-sewn garments, one loincloth and another upper-body cloth. The Messenger of Allah (blessings and peace be upon him) was asked what one should wear during Hajj, and he said: "Do not wear a long shirt or a turban or pants or a cloak or leather shoes – except for someone who doesnt have sandals in which case he can wear leather shoes that are cut below the ankles, and do not wear any clothes died with saffron or red dye".

Forty First Lesson

Rules pertaining to errors in Hajj

Whoever missed or neglected one of the essential integrals of Hajj then he should not release himself from the state of Ihram until he performs that integral and offers a sacrifice in the sacred precinct. If he misses the standing at 'Arafa, he should perform an 'Umrah.

Whoever missed or neglected one of the obligatory elements then he must sacrifice a sheep in the sacred precinct, and if unable then he should fast 3 days before the end of Hajj and 7 days back at home.

Whoever performs something prohibited during Ihram he must atone by offering a sacrifice with its meat given as charity to the poor or by giving 9 liters of food to six poor people. Whoever cuts a tree in the sacred precinct then he should atone by sacrificing a cow (if the tree is big) or a sheep (if the tree is small). Whoever hunts game during Hajj, then he should sacrifice a similar animal and give its meat as charity or an equivalent value in wealth.

The circling around the Ka'ba has conditions as follows:
- being pure of ritual and physical impurity
- covering one's nakedness
- beginning the circuit at the black stone with the left shoulder facing in line with it

The conditions of going between Safa and Marwa (called Sa'i) are:
- that it occur after a complete 7 rounds around the Ka'ba
- that one begins from Safa first and ends with Marwa
- that one does each leg seven times total

Allah said: *"Indeed, Safa and Marwa are from the sacred rites of Allah"* (Q2:158).

There are three ways of doing Hajj, and the specific type should be included in the intention:
- Ifrad: which is to perform Hajj only without an Umrah
- Qiran: which is to perform both Hajj and Umrah together with one state of Ihram
- Tamattu': which is to perform Umrah first with one Ihram, then release from Ihram, then perform a Hajj

Forty Second Lesson

the necessity of visiting the Prophet (blessings and peace upon him)

Everyone who does pilgrimage should also make their way to Madina for the purpose of visiting the Prophet (blessings and peace be upon him), whether he does that before or after Hajj, so that he may find a place for himself in Paradise. The Messenger of Allah (blessings and peace be upon him) has said: "Whoever performs Hajj and does not come to visit me, then he has treated me rudely". He also taught us that we should not intend to travel to any mosque except three: the Sacred Mosque in Makka, the Prophet's Mosque in Madina, and the Aqsa Mosque in Palestine.

* * *

BOOK II

Motherly Advices for Muslim Girls Concerning Religious and Worldly Life

Introduction

In the Name of Allah the Universally Merciful and Singularly Compassionate, may the blessings and peace of Allah be upon our master Muhammad and his family and companions…Amen!

After an extensive time of teaching and rearing young girls about religion, I was inspired to write down some points of advice and counsel that will insha'Allah be of benefit to them. I have attempted to support my words with well known and established principles of Islam using references from the Qur'an and Prophetic narrations. I have named this letter:

Motherly Advice for the Muslim Girl
Concerning Religious and Worldly Life

I will insha'Allah follow it up with a second piece, and I ask the readers – men and women – to look upon this letter with the eye of good pleasure, and that they constructively point me towards any error that I may correct it. I ask Allah the Most High to accept this from me and to cause this work to guide and benefit even if just one lady, that I may find supreme success with Allah!

Ruqayya, daughter of Shaykh al-Islam

City of Kawlakh, 9/12/1383 H.

* * *

First Advice

O dear respectful girl, you should try your best to maintain good character with your parents, especially your mother. For the father is the one who exerts himself throughout the day and toils hard in acquiring daily provision to spend upon the daughter and fulfill her needs as long as she is vulnerable. As for the mother, she carried her for 9 months and breastfed her for two years, staying awake to ensure her comfort and worried lest any sickness or ailment beset her. She cleans and washes off any filth and impurity, that being more desirous to her heart than everything else. Allah Himself has counseled us in the Qur'an to show respect to the parents, stressing the importance of that by saying:

"And your Lord has decreed that you worship none but Him and that you deal excellently with both of your parents. If one or both of them reach old age with you, you should not say to them even "Uff" nor humiliate them, but rather keep your speech with them noble. Lower the wings of humility before them out of mercy and say, 'O Lord have mercy on them for they reared me when I was little'" (**Q17:23-24**).

The Messenger – upon him be blessings and peace – emphasized the mandatory duty of respectful kindness to one's mother in a special way, when one of the Muslims asked him, "Who is most deserving of my good dealings with them?" and he responded, 'your mother' (3 times). He asked, "then who?" He answered, 'your father'. It was also authentically recorded that he – upon him blessings and peace – said, "Paradise lies under the feet of the mother".

* * *

Second Advice

O dear Muslim girl, when you awake from sleep in the sixth hour of the morning then rise up from your bed with comportment and praise Allah Most High for maintaining your health. Head over to the restroom to wash yourself, then tidy up the house without delay; so you straighten or replace the bed sheets and fluff the pillows and clean the floors of the house.

At that moment should come the preferred time for the Subh prayer, at which point you should perform the ablution for Salat as you learned in school, and do not instead perform tayammum without an excuse out of laziness as other heedless girls do. Then you perform the Subh prayer along with the sunna prayer before it, and after that head over to your mother to greet her with the greeting of Islam which is: "As salamu 'alaykum", and then to your father. If you wish to add more you can say: "As salamu 'alaykum wa rahmatullah" (Peace be upon you and the mercy of Allah).

After that you should wear your day clothes and brush and clean your teeth and comb your hair, and wear your bracelets and ring and necklace and jewelry, and cover your entire body with clothes except for your face and hands. Then drink some coffee and eat some breakfast, and ask permission to go over to girls school, where you learn the sciences of the Qur'an and the religion, as well as sewing and knitting and other household skills useful for women.

* * *

Third Advice

The importance of amicable dealings with people: The Messenger of Allah – blessings and peace be upon him – said: "The people having the worst position with Allah on the Day of Judgment are those whom other people avoid because of their obscene behavior".

So dear Muslim girl, observe good character in dealings with people and make your words gentle without meekness in a way that engenders positive connections with them, but taking care not to appear too easy and flirtatious with men. In the Qur'an Allah Most High taught the Messenger – upon him be blessings and peace – how to interact with the people and engender their love for him, by saying: *"It was by mercy from Allah that you were gentle with them, and if you were rough and hard of heart they would have dissipated from your company; so overlook their errors and ask Divine forgiveness for them, and consult with them in the community affairs."* **(Q3:159)**.

He – may blessings of Allah and peace be upon him – also stated, "Whoever does not show mercy will not be shown mercy." Therefore accustom yourself to have mercy for the young and respect for the old.

* * *

Fourth Advice

After your return from the school, you should rest for a time sufficient to eat your lunch, then without delay clean the pots and dishes and utensils and so on, before the Dhuhr prayer. Once the adhan for the Dhuhr prayer is called, then ensure you perform it in the beginning of its time so that you can be able to return to the school. As for during days off school, you can visit one's older siblings and aunts and relatives, as time permits, to maintain family ties.

As has been mentioned in the hadiths, the family ties are attached to the legs of the Divine Throne, saying: "O Allah, connect those who maintain my connection and sever those who sever my connection". Similarly, these visits uphold positive relations and keep away arguments and ill feelings. We find in the hadith: "Should I inform you of something of higher stature than fasting and charity and prayer?" The companions said, 'yes of course!' He said, "It is to foster healthy relationships, for corrupted relationships is the 'Shaver'. I do not mean that it shaves hair but that it shaves away the Din".

He – blessings and peace be upon him – also said, "The rights of a Muslim over another are six:

1) If he greets you to return his greeting
2) If he invites you to answer his invitation
3) If he asks for advice to advise him sincerely
4) If he sneezes and praises Allah to bless him
5) If he falls ill to visit him
6) If he died to attend his funeral.

* * *

Fifth Advice

The necessity of chastity for Muslim girls: It is beneficial for you to not frequently spend time out of the house here and there, because that is forbidden in the Shari'ah as Allah stated: *"Remain in your homes and do not flaunt yourselves in the manner of the former culture of ignorance…"* **(Q33:33).**

Avoid being alone with non-related (*mahram*) males, and do not unnecessarily speak too much, for too much useless talk is unbecoming, especially for a lady. Do not as well make mention of the faults of others, for the Messenger – blessings and peace be upon him – said: "The Muslim is the one from whose tongue and hand other Muslims are safe".

Do not reveal your private parts, and as you have learned a woman's private parts include her whole body except her face and hands. Also, do not become used to sitting regularly with mothers in their circles, for that might lead to hearing one of their secrets, which you would then reveal to your siblings and friends.

After completing your education at school you should learn how to cook and clean and iron clothes, and accustom yourself to a clean environment and setting the table and welcoming guests whenever they show up, by returning their greetings and saying "welcome enter among family and friends". Then prepare some refreshments for them in clean cups and present it to them with good manners, not staring at them to see how they drink. Rather, look elsewhere such as towards the ground. When they return the cup, you should ask them if you can offer more.

You should also be intimately familiar with the example of the wives of the Prophet and the noble women of the first generations of Islam – may Allah be pleased with them – who knew how to read and write and were scholars of the religion… such as Hafsah bint Umar, and A'isha bint Abu Bakr (may Allah be pleased with them). She was an amazing example, for she would teach recitation of Qur'an and religious knowledge, such that the Prophet – blessings and peace be upon him – would say about her: "Take half of your religion from this young lady". Urwa ibn Zubayr said of her: "I have not seen anyone more knowledgeable of fiqh or medicine or poetry than A'isha". She transmitted from the Prophet – blessings and peace be upon him – more than (two) thousand hadith.

Therefore, do not diminish the importance of emulating these noble women who are our mothers. Among them also is Sukayna bint al-Husayn, famous for her knowledge, bravery, trustworthiness, and loyalty. I am only telling you all of this to make you aware that you have equal access to the states of perfection as males do. Islam equalizes the men and women, and Allah has obligated the seeking of knowledge upon all Muslims, male and female, so beware of neglecting half of the Ummah of Sayyidina Muhammad (blessings of Allah and His peace on him).

* * *

Sixth Advice

Concerning Hygiene and Daily Manners: O dear Muslim girl, you should avoid anything which carries harmful bacteria because it could lead to various illnesses, such as mosquitoes landing on your food or drink. Do not buy any food sold by outside vendors who walk around on the streets because it could harm one's health. Also, you should consider having your own belongings that others will not use, such as your own drinking cup, towel, toothbrush and toothpaste, bed and pillow, and so on. Drink clean pure water, and do so in sips and not in gulps, because gulping water leads to liver ailment as is mentioned in the Hadith.

Among the manners of eating is that you wash your hands before and after eating your meal, in accordance with Prophetic practice. If you sit with others on a table of food, do not begin eating before those who are greater in age or status than you. Do not eat more than your present need for food, and do not covet food that isn't directly before you. Begin eating with invoking the Name of Allah, and after finishing praise Him. Do not show disgust with a food nor should you be glutinous. Do not stuff your mouth full of food, and chew the food well before swallowing.

When in the house, do not annoy the others with boisterous play, and do not toy with and mess up the house appliances or draw or write on the walls. If the house has an attached garden, do not play with the flowers or shrubs. Also, take care of forgetting to honor your parents while in the house as we mentioned in the first advice. Rather, implement what they request of you, and sit respectfully in their presence. When you see one of them approach, you should stand respectfully to greet them, and you should not raise your voice above theirs. Do what you can to please them and avoid angering them. You should also honor their reputation when with others, by not for example insulting the parents of others which would lead to them retaliating by insulting your parents. Rather, avoid bad language entirely.

* * *

Seventh Advice

Concerning having good dealing with siblings: The young Muslim lady should treat her younger siblings nicely and mercifully, and should not annoy them or take anything from them without their permission, for that would lead to the anger of her parents and shows a great blemish in the manners of the young lady. She should always treat her siblings gently and with good manners.

She should also respect her relatives, including her uncles and aunts and cousins, because they are related to her parents and they love her and wish for her ease and success. In addition, she should also deal respectfully with any guests in the home of her parents, showing them gentleness and smiles and easy temperament. She should never annoy the servants or neighbors. That would indicate deficiency in intellect and poor upbringing…

* * *

Eighth Advice

Concerning good manners with neighbors: This is one of the most important responsibilities of young Muslim ladies. You should take it seriously, for the Prophet – blessings and peace be upon him – said, "Jibril continued to remind me about the importance of treating neighbors well until I thought he would include them among the recipients of one's inheritance", meaning that they would have a right to a portion of the inheritance by law. In another case, he – blessings and peace be upon him – said, "None of you will achieve full Iman until he loves for his brother what he loves for himself".

Among the examples of good manners with one's neighbors is that one removes any harm or annoyance from them or their children, and that you greet them whenever you see them or pass by, and visit them when they fall ill, and also during special occasions. You should never refuse to provide them small acts of kindness, which include daily articles that people borrow from each other.

Do not ever humiliate a poor person for their poverty, nor anyone with a physical flaw, nor make fun of them. Rather you should praise Allah with thanks for keeping you free of that which He tested others.

Whenever you come to your neighbor's house, you should ask permission to enter. This is your obligation even if he is the closest of people to you. Someone asked the Prophet (blessings and peace of Allah upon him), "Should I ask permission to enter upon my mother?" and he said "Yes you should". He further asked him, "What if I serve her and am constantly going back and forth, should I still ask every time?" and he replied, "Would you like to accidently see her unclothed?" He said, "No of course not". So the Prophet said, "Then you should request permission each time before entering".

Allah Most High stated, *"O you who believe! Do not enter houses that are not yours until you seek permission to enter and offer greetings to their inhabitants, that is superior for you so that you may take heed before acting. If you do not find anyone inside them then do not enter until you obtain clear permission... and Allah is knowledgeable of all that you do"* (**Q24:27-28**).

The number of times to request permission to enter is three times maximum, in accordance with the Prophet's words (blessings and peace be upon him): "If one of you asks permission three times to enter and is not granted permission, then he should return back". All of these are vital manners for the Muslim young lady, because later she will become a mother and be responsible for raising children.

* * *

Ninth Advice

Concerning the engagement period and what follows it: When you reach the age of marriage and find the physical and emotional signs indicating that, and when men begin to show interest in you, you must be careful not to act flirtatiously and reveal your beauty before men. This is not permitted in the Shari'ah and is unbecoming to the nobility of Muslim women. Allah Most High said: "*O Prophet! Inform your wives and daughters and the believing women that they should draw their shawls close to them, that they should be recognized and hence not teased, and Allah is Forgiving and Merciful*" (**Q33:59**).

If Allah decrees marriage at that time – which is the most important thing in the life of a woman – then be careful not to overburden your husband with numerous requests. The only financial duty that the Shari'ah has obligated upon the husband towards the wife is the dowry, as Allah said: "*Pay to the women their due dowry in the spirit of a gift*" (**Q4:4**), because the free woman is not bought or sold. Only the dowry is given in accordance to the Qur'an and Sunnah. Likewise, the husband is obligated to provide for the family's daily expenditures, including food and clothing and appropriate dwelling, as Allah stated: "*Men are the caretakers of women*" (**Q4:34**) and "*Let the affluent spend from his wealth (upon his spouse and family)*" (**Q65:7**). The Messenger – upon him be blessings and peace – said: "The right of the woman upon her spouse is that he feeds her and clothe her and not strike her or abuse her…"

O dear Muslim lady, rise to the occasion and be earnest in dealing well with your husband, and know that you have rights owed to you as well as obligations due from you in your relationship with him. Allah said to the husbands, "*Live with them in kindness*" (**Q4:19**) and "*They have similar rights as you have other them*" (**Q2:228**). The Messenger – blessings and peace be upon him – said, "Treat your women well for they are entrusted to you" and "The best of you are those who are best to their women and daughters, and the most virtuous of the believers are the ones with the best character".

So you should interact with your husband and his family and children and friends with good manners, just as he is required to live with you amiably and kindly with respect and care, and lead you to the straight path; otherwise he has betrayed you and betrayed the religion. The Messenger – blessings and peace be upon him – said: "Be cognizant of Allah when dealing with women, for they are entrusted to you, so whoever does not encourage the women of his house to pray nor teach them the required religious knowledge then he has betrayed Allah and His Messenger".

* * *

Tenth Advice

Concerning the rights of the husband: As long as you are with your husband, you must obey him and not interrupt him when he speaks and stand when he approaches and show happiness when you see him and apply perfume for him and wear clean clothes. You should be satisfied with what Allah provided him. Do not exit the house without his permission, and not invite into the house whom he does not want, and if he invites righteous guests you should show them good manners. Stand by his side helping him in difficult times and be with him during the good and bad.

You should also deal nicely and gently with the servants, and not speak harshly with them or curse them, as other dimwitted women do. This could lead to others emulating that bad behavior, for the children listen to and copy you, and the mother is a school for the children.

The wife should only consider splitting the bond from her husband after exercising patience, in such situations for example if the husband is clearly unable to provide for the wife or clothe her or find a suitable dwelling, or if one of the spouses is barren because reproduction is important for the married couple. In cases such as these then it is permitted for the wife to separate and undo the marriage bond. Otherwise, it is a disgrace upon you O Muslim lady for you to request a divorce from your husband without a reasonable cause, and the Prophet (blessings and peace upon him) gave a stern warning against such a thing, when he said: "Any woman who needlessly requests divorce from her husband without their being any fault, then the fragrance of Paradise is forbidden for her". Abu Bakr as-Siddiq said, 'I heard the Messenger of Allah (blessings and peace upon him) say: "If a wife says to her husband Divorce me (without valid cause), then she will come on the Day of Resurrection with her face having no flesh and her tongue hanging from the back of her neck, and she will fall into the pit of Hell, even if she used to fast during the day and pray during the night".

* * *

Eleventh Advice

On the necessity of patience: It is important for you O Muslim lady to have patience with the difficulties of daily life, following the example of the mother of noble ones Fatima Zahra (Allah be pleased with her). She used to pound and kneed the wheat grains until it affected her honorable hands, and draw and carry well water until it left a mark on her neck, and clean the house and cook food until it stained her clothes, and in all of this maintained the worship of Allah until He became pleased with her.

When this lifestyle became hard to bear for her she complained to her father the noble Prophet and asked for a house servant to help her, he denied the request and indicated something more useful for her, namely that she glorify Allah 33 times and praise Him 33 times and magnify Him 34 times when going to bed, and when she prays the dawn and sunset prayers to say 10 times "*la ilaha illa Allah wahdahu la sharika lahu lahu'l mulk wa lahu'l hamd yuhyi wa yumit bi Yadihi'l khayr wa huwa 'ala kulli shay'in qadir*". Each one of those ten times would count as ten good deeds recorded and ten bad deeds erased and emancipating one slave, and no harm satanic or otherwise would be able to touch her.

So in this noble righteous mother you have a great example O young Muslim lady; this daughter of the Messenger of Allah (upon them be blessings and peace) whose bedcover – when she wed Sayyidina Ali – consisted of sheepskin that was not long enough to cover both their feet. She was the master of all women, and she knew that this life is temporary and the next life is permanent.

Here is a story for you to consider: It is narrated that the Prophet came to her house one day (blessings and peace of Allah upon them) and found an embroidered cloth on her door and decided not to enter. When Sayyidina Ali (Allah be pleased with him) later came, he found her worried and asked what the matter was. She said, "The Prophet came and didn't enter". He came to the Prophet and said, "O Messenger of Allah, Fatima is uneasy that you came to our house but did not enter". He replied, "And what connection do I have with the lower world (*dunya*) and what do I have to do with designs and embroidery?" The design was in the shape of a human figure. So Ali came to Fatima and informed her of the Prophet's reply and she said, "What would he have me do with it?" He said, "Let her send it as a gift to so-and-so", and it was mentioned that it was the Ahl as-Suffa. I say: Such indeed is the mother of noble ones and the master of all women in this life and the next.

As for the injustice that some men practice towards women then do not ever be satisfied or complicit with that at all, such as if he spends more time with your co-wife disregarding the required alternations, or does not give equal distribution of money or gifts, or other such examples. In all of that, never accept to remain in the house as something hanging mid-air for this is humiliating for you, and the wife is equal to the husband. If it reaches to where he stops providing for you then it is permitted – as we mentioned above – to seek divorce. This also applies if the husband demands too much work from his wife day and night, for this is unfitting for her physiology, and the man shouldn't forget his position of caretaker for her.

The Messenger (blessings and peace be upon him) said: "Only a noble man treats women nobly, and only an ignoble man treats women poorly". The Prophet – blessings and peace upon him – ordered the men to take into consideration the unique nature of women when dealing kindly with them, for the woman was created from a curved rib which cannot be straightened and isn't meant to. If he tries to then straighten it he will end up cracking it – meaning it would lead to divorce because abandoning her nature would be unbearable. The husband should also keep himself attractive for his wife, as the Prophet (blessings and peace upon him) advised them: "Wash your clothes, trim your hair, brush your teeth, keep clean and dress well; for when the men of Bani Israel did not do that, their women began having illicit affairs".

* * *

Twelfth and Final Advice

You should take care to avoid all blameworthy traits and acts, such as lying, tale-bearing, gossiping, spying, arrogance, envy, miserliness, and so on, for all of these are the greatest stains upon a woman, and Allah Most High has forbidden them, saying: *"And do not spy upon one another nor backbite, would one of you enjoy eating the dead flesh of his brother?"* **(Q49:12)** and He said, *"And do not comply with every vain swearing one, backbiter, going around with slander, hinderer of good, guilty aggressor, coarse mannered…"* **(Q68:10-12)**. And the Prophet (blessings and peace upon him) said: "The two faced one will have no face with Allah".

Here is another story for you to ponder: A woman came to the Prophet (upon him be blessings and peace) to ask him a question about her situation, and when she left A'isha said, "my she is short" and he replied, "Beware of gossip!" She said, "I only characterized her with a quality she already has" He replied, "True and that is gossip, and if you said something she didn't have it would be slander".

Additionally, you should avoid miserliness because it is forbidden in Shari'ah, and Allah said *"whoever hoards gold and silver and does not spend them in the Way of Allah then warn them of painful torment, the Day when (that money) will be heated in the fire of Hell and branded into their foreheads and sides and backs, it being said to them 'this is the wealth you hoarded for yourselves, so taste now what you used to hoard'"* **(Q9:34-35)**.

Concerning the blameworthiness of lying He Most High said: "*It is only those who disbelieve in the signs of Allah that concoct lies, and those indeed are the true liars*" **(Q16:105)**. About forbidding envy the Prophet (blessings and peace upon him) said: "Do not envy one another, do not hate one another, do not plot against one another, but be true brothers O servants of Allah".

* * *

Conclusion

O dear Muslim lady, these are some motherly advices concerning religion and manners which I quickly wrote for you out of love to serve you and serve the Din, and the Din is all advice as stated in the hadith. And Allah do I ask to accept this work as sincere service for His sake, and that He facilitate for me to write a second sequel which would be larger and more beneficial, and that He inspire my Muslim sisters with right guidance and avidity to uphold the obligations of Muslim women, until they themselves turn to composing and writing helpful books, and this is not difficult for Allah.

May the eternal blessings and peace of Allah be upon our Master Muhammad and his household and companions!

* * *

This Book was finished on the eve of Friday the 9th Day of Dhu'l Hijja

In the year 1383 Hijra in the City of Kawlakh in the Republic of Senegal,

Hoping that Allah Most High will confirm it as a good deed in this life and

the Next, and He is Capable of that and that is not difficult for Him!

When Sahib al Fayda Shaykh al Islam al-Haj Ibrahim Niass read over this book of mine, he offered this compliment:

"Praise and thanks belongs to Allah, and whatever blessing you have comes from Allah, and my success is only through Allah, and there is no power or ability except by Allah, and may the Divine blessings and peace be upon the best of the creation of Allah, Sayyidina Muhammad ibn Abdillah the Messenger of Allah. O dear righteous daughter Sayida Ruqayya! I have read your letter, praising Allah for the blessing of your existence and the blessing of His support of you, and I ask Him Most High to accept your efforts and bring happiness in your life and in the life of all who work towards propagating this work whether male or female. May He always keep you in His protection! Peace be upon you!"

Your father Ibrahim.

* * *

Praise belongs to Allah! This small book of mine was examined by many righteous scholars in this country, those of high moral character and sharp intellects, all of them embarrassing me with their laudation. My expectation is that they would encourage me to continue writing. I have gratitude for all of them, and I ask their pardon for not being able to reproduce all of their written compliments. I have here given examples of some of them, because short letters such as these are not the place for long appendices of compliments.

The representative and confidant of the Shaykh Ali Ya Siin ibn al-Hasan wrote the following:

"All Praise belongs to Allah Who bore witness - along with the angels and the upright scholars - that there is no god but He, the Mighty the Wise; indeed, the Din acceptable to Allah is Islam! And Divine blessings and peace upon the example for all mankind, Sayyidina Muhammad, the manifest proof and criterion of truth, and upon his household and companions!

I examined the "Motherly Advice" written by the righteous and knowledgeable lady of lofty aspirations, the Muqaddama Haja Ruqayya daughter of Shaykh al-Islam Mawlana Hajj Ibrahim (may Allah benefit us through him). When I grazed in the gardens of these advices and delved closely into their meanings, I found them to be an exposition of numerous pleasing manners, securing success for the righteous believing young ladies. How could it not be so, when it selected the loftiest pearls and the most beneficial teachings. This demonstrates that this exceptional lady has herself acquired these noble traits. It is said that the best blessings upon a person are to be granted sound intellect and high morals, which guarantee the excellence demanded in this life and the next. Indeed, the author of these advices already demonstrated her rank by her previous speeches and lordly teachings... may Allah increase her mentally and physically, by the honor of the pivot of all knowledge and understanding!"

- The servant of the Ibrahimi Presence, Ali Ya Siin ibn al-Hasan, may Allah be kind to him!

**

The Ustadh Muhammad al-Kabir ibn Alawi al-Mauritani wrote this compliment:

> "The Advice of this young lady revealed true guidance -
>
> in turn guiding her to the loftiest state.
>
> By it do the ladies of this time rise up -
>
> if they acquire the traits and manners here mentioned.
>
> Within its pages the words shine forth -
>
> expertly arranged, clarifying all confusions.
>
> Lines of words which dispel darkness -
>
> bringing with them clear Divine verses.
>
> Ruqayya you have brought forth a useful book -
>
> benefiting the believing muslim women.
>
> You emulated the Shaykh, and he is your father indeed -
>
> and your Shaykh, so take from him and give (us)
>
> How many miracles did he show to us -
>
> and you indeed are some of those miracles!"

* * *

The Ustadh Ibrahim Mahmud Jub, the secretary-general of Ansar ad-Din organization and the special confidant of my father Shaykh al-Islam Haj Ibrahim Niass, wrote a long compliment which included the following:

"I won't forget the time when you took first place in the grammar class at school and your father nicknamed you "the Young Lady of the City" and gifted you with an expensive pure gold coin, and I considered the nickname and the gold coin as a mark of honor with which your father the Shaykh expressed his appreciation for your efforts. Today you continue to work in the field of knowledge and prepare yourself for the future role of giving guidance and direction. At this time, after all those fruitful years, I ask your permission to nickname you "The Young Lady Leader", because by virtue of this book you are indeed a respected leader to our young Muslim girls in all of Western Africa as far as I know. You did the preparatory work and now became unique in your position, showing your trust in Allah Who grants victory to the sincere, convinced of the need for the woman to struggle side-by-side with the man in service and in life. Now we see that you gift the Arabic readers among the Muslims in general, and the young Muslima girls in particular, the first Arabic composition by a Muslim lady from Black Africa. So accept O Young Leader my warmest congratulations for your great achievements.

"There is no need for me to follow the example of other complimenters by mentioning specific quotes from your book, because the entire work is deserving of quotation... How can it not be so, when it is - as the Khadim of the Ibrahimi Presence said - a gathering of the loftiest pearls and most beneficial teachings? Indeed he spoke the truth, for what pearls are loftier than the manners of spiritual striving that Islam came with, and what teaching is more beneficial than the noble character traits sent with and perfected by our master Muhammad (blessings and peace be upon him)? Therefore this book is nothing less than a shining torch of the Islamic manners.

"*Allah Most High said: 'The believing men and women are supporting friends to each other, they command the good and forbid the evil, establish the salat and pay the zakat, and obey Allah and His Messenger, these Allah will show mercy, and indeed Allah is Mighty and Wise'* **(Q9:71)**; and He said *'The hypocrites men and women come from each other, they command the evil and forbid the good and cling their hands in miserliness, they neglected Allah so He neglected them, indeed the hypocrites are the corrupt sinners'.* **(Q9:67).**

"You have been truthful O Young Lady Leader, for the equality between the spouses in Islam is a reality which none argues against except an ignorant or arrogant one, because the responsibility for commanding good and forbidding evil is the greatest responsibility in Islam, and these verses could not be clearer in stating the equal responsibility upon males and females to that task. To Allah belongs all praise, and congratulations to you for understanding your religion and knowing that the balance of life does not occur without the woman fulfilling her responsibilities completely without failure or lazy dependence upon others. May Allah preserve you and continue to grant you success and happiness…Ameen!"

* * *

The noble Shaykh Haj al-Hasan ibn Muhammad al-Fuli wrote the following:

"Praise belongs to Allah Who shines the lights of Divine knowledge and Eternal wisdom, and blessings and peace be upon the secret of the universal form and never-ending meanings, our master Muhammad the Messenger of Allah!

"I read over the composition of the noble lady, descendent of the upright scholars and righteous saints, Haja Ruqayya daughter of the Shaykh Ibrahim Niass, which she entitled "Motherly Advices Concerning Life and Religion", and I found it to be a composition which matches its title, woven with Qur'anic verses and authentic Prophetic statements, displayed in the utmost manner of eloquence. Indeed she gave sincere counsel to men and women young and old, may Allah increase her like in the Muhammadan Ummah and bless her. May Allah make this book a cause of full acceptance and continual approach and of benefit to everyone...Ameen!"

* * *

The Ustadh Muhammad Amin Ibrahim Niass expressed his admiration of this book, writing:

> "Ruqayya you achieved nobility and honor -
>
> and surpassed the men of the town in high rank.
>
> By the "Advice to the Girls" you acquired a station -
>
> which continues to dispel ignorance
>
> Your prose is like a stringed array of pearls -
>
> likewise in your poetry is seen no loss of words

We hope in the Generous Master and His bounty -

by the honor of the Prophet that it benefits all

And that by virtue of this book a new generation -

is formed who yearn for the sublime Sunna

And He preserve the Lady of the Village as an honor for our land -

honoring her further and showing us the way by her

By the high rank of the Messenger of Allah, supporter of His Din -

and all his companions and those who emulate the Messengers

May the Blessings of Allah be upon him as long as an admirer says

-

Ruqayya you have achieved nobility and honor!"

* * *

www.ingramcontent.com/pod-product-compliance
Lightning Source LLC
Chambersburg PA
CBHW070632300426
44113CB00010B/1748